THE LOCKDOWN DRILL

Written by Lieutenant Becky Coyle

Illustrated by juanbjuan oliver

An Introduction to Lockdown Drills and School Safety

SCHOOL SAFETY

School Resource Officer Approved

Dedicated to the Williamson County Sheriff's Department SRO Division, Williamson County Schools, and to Kinsley, Dallas, Thea, and Marley Rose.

Special thank you to Mrs. Maggi Margaret Turner, who made this book project possible.

—Becky

www.FlowerpotPress.com
PAB-0909-0375
ISBN: 978-1-4867-3006-3
Made in China/Fabriqué en Chine

Hi, my name is Becky. I am a police lieutenant and school resource officer. I love teaching children just like you the importance of being safe while they are playing and learning at school.

Sometimes it is hard to understand why you have to practice drills and follow school rules, but being prepared is an important part of keeping your school safe. Your teachers, school officer, classmates, and even YOU play an important role in ensuring that your school is a place where you can do all of the things that you love to do! By working together and following the rules, we can accomplish so much!

For more information, discussion topics, and activities, visit my website!

www.Cops4Schools.com.

Stay safe,
Lieutenant Becky Coyle

Why are there officers that work in our schools?

Is it to arrest us for breaking the rules?

NO! It's to protect us and teach safety, too.

When they teach lockdown drills, we'll know what to do!

The class was getting ready to put on a magic show.

They had practiced it all week and were now set up to go!

"Excuse the interruption. Could you listen and be still?

We would like to run a test of our school-wide lockdown drill!

Now quickly everybody, hurry up and find your space.

Remember to stay quiet as we hustle into place."

So Finn grabbed his lizard Fred, then he got them both in line.

"Just stay really quiet, Fred, and I'm sure that you'll be fine."

Somebody started pushing as they squished in super tight!

Then the room got really dark when Ms. Crum turned off the light.

Fred's breath was pretty stinky, which made Finn scrunch up his nose.

And then he started fussing when JT sat on his toes.

And Ming kept right on talking, saying, "Someone pick a card!"

Miguel started complaining. He said, "Handcuff tricks are hard!"

Rebekah flashed her gold coin. "Watch me make it disappear!

And with a bit of magic, pull it out of Jack's right ear!"

The noise kept getting louder. It seemed no one could stay still.

Ms. Crum said, "PLEASE BE QUIET WHEN YOU'RE IN A LOCKDOWN DRILL!"

At last they all were quiet, that's when Maya turned around.
    She pointed toward the vacuum. "Take a look at what I found!"
The big, bright red square button had caught little Maya's eye.
    The button did say PUSH ME, so she felt she HAD to try!
That's when Finn saw her reaching and he whispered, "Maya, NOOOOOO!
    Please do not push that button!" But Finn was a bit too slow.
As Maya pushed the button, Finn leapt up and crossed the room,
    but not in time to stop her. Then he heard the vacuum...VROOOOM!

PUSH
ME

VROOOOOOM

When the vacuum made a roar, it was just too much for Fred,
so he jumped out of Finn's hat and landed right on Maya's head!
That made Maya scream out loud, and it made the whole class jump,
which brought noise from all over...a BIG BOOM...a CLANG...a BUMP!

clang!

That caused even more screaming and then everybody ran!
Nothing in this lockdown drill went according to the plan.

The officer reviewed with them so next time they'd do better.

He said they'd all do great if they tried hard to work together!

"Why do we practice lockdown drills and practice how to hide?

It's for special emergencies when we all stay inside.

This almost NEVER happens, but we practice just in case.

The practice makes us faster as we get to our safe place.

Just like when we drill for fires or another safety test,

we practice our reactions so we can all do our best!"

And then they got to try again and try with all their might!

No booms, or clangs, or bumps this time—they got it all just right!

They even found a log for Fred with a small space inside.

Now Fred can practice lockdowns too with his new place to hide!

"See you tomorrow!"